A Voice From North-Carolina. The Secessionists

Richard Spaight Donnell, supposed author

A

VOICE FROM NORTH-CAROLINA.

THE

SECESSIONISTS:

HEIR PROMISES AND PERFORMANCES; THE CONDITION
INTO WHICH THEY HAVE BROUGHT THE COUN-
TRY; THE REMEDY, ETC.

REPRINTED FROM THE RALEIGH (N. C.) STANDARD, OF JULY 31, 1863.

* ● *

NEW-YORK:
ANSON D. F. RANDOLPH,
683 BROADWAY.
1863.

The following remarkable article, which appeared in the Raleigh (N. C.) Standard, on July thirty-first, is reported to have been written by Hon. R. S. Donnell, Speaker of the House of Commons of North-Carolina, aided by F. B. Satterthwaite, President of the Governor's Council, and to have been published with the approval of Gov. Vance. We publish the article, and italicize, etc., as it was printed in the Standard.

THE SECESSIONISTS:

THEIR PROMISES AND PERFORMANCES; THE CONDITION INTO WHICH THEY HAVE BROUGHT THE COUNTRY; THE REMEDY, ETC.

No War Analogous to this.

MR. EDITOR: There is, so far as I remember, no war to be met with in history entirely analogous to the one now raging between the North and the South. That produced by an attempt on the part of three of the Swiss Cantons to separate themselves from the Confederation, a few years since, in some respects, resembles it most nearly. That attempt, it will be remembered, was arrested, and the rebellious Cantons speedily reduced to submission by the arms of the Confederacy. It is frequently compared to our old Revolutionary struggle with the mother country, but there is scarcely an analogy between the two cases. The thirteen Colonies were not like the Southern

States, equal in political rights with the other States of the British Empire. They possessed no sovereign power whatever. They were not, as we were, entitled to representation in the common Parliament of the British Union, but were mere colonies — mere dependencies upon the mother country. In an evil hour the administration of George Grenville, and afterwards that of Lord North, attempted to impose a tax upon the Colonies. This oppression was resisted, and the resistance was made the pretext for other oppressions more unjust still. The Colonies continued their resistance in a constitutional way for nearly ten years, by representations, remonstrances, and petitions for the redress of grievances; but all in vain. At length they took up arms, with the avowed object of enforcing such redress.

The Colonies did not seek Separation.

They solemnly *disclaimed all* intention of separation from the parent State, for they were as loyal in their feelings of attachment to the British Constitution as were the inhabitants of Surrey or Cornwall. This resolute step they confidently expected would procure the desired·redress; but the advice of all the ablest statesmen of that age — of Chatham, of Camden, of Burke, of Fox, of Rockingham, and others, were thrown away upon the narrow-minded monarch and the bigoted ministry which then swayed the destinies of the British Empire. Still in hope, they continued the struggle for one whole year: At length the British Parliament declared the Colonies out of the protection of the parent State. And then at last, no· other course was left them but to proclaim their independ-ence, and defend it, if need be, with their life's blood. The battle of Lexington was fought on the nineteenth of April, 1775, and on the twelfth of April, 1776, the Provincial Congress of. North-Carolina "empowered their delegates in Congress to concur with the dele-gates of the other Colonies in declaring independence and forming foreign alliances," and on the fifteenth of the following month, Virginia, through her Conven-tion, instructed her delegates in the Continental Con-gress "to propose to that body to declare the United Colonies free and independent States, absolved from all allegiance to, or dependence on, the Crown or Parlia-ment of Great Britain," and on the Fourth of July following the ever memorable Declaration was made.

The Course of the Secessionists.

But how different has been the course of the Seces-sionists! They seem to have resolved years ago that the Union *should* be destroyed, and then to have set themselves to work to *forge* such grievances as would seem to give them a decent pretext for the accomplish-ment of their premeditated schemes. The first effort was made in the days of nullification by the Secession-ists of South-Carolina. The grievance then complained of was the tariff, although the State of South-Carolina, herself, had been, from the foundation of the Govern-ment nearly up to that period, as strong an advocate of a high tariff as any State in New-England. That question was compromised — South-Carolina obtained all that she *ostensibly* demanded. A revenue tariff, with incidental protection, became the settled policy of the Government, and, except for a short period under the tariff of 1842, was never departed from. But still they were not satisfied.

The Slave Question.

Immediately after the passage of Mr. Clay's Compromise bill, the newspaper organ of the Secessionists at Washington declared: " That *the South could never be united on the tariff question,* and that the *slave question* was the only one that could unite them." And Mr. Calhoun, if I mistake not, said the same thing in a speech at Abbeville, in South-Carolina, about the same time; and of course was followed by all the lesser lights among his adherents. Then commenced that violent agitation of the Slavery question which had nearly culminated upon the admission of California, in 1850. Again, by the efforts of those immortal statesmen of the last age, Messrs. Webster, Clay, and others, was the matter compromised. The whole country at first appeared to be satisfied with the settlement, but it soon appeared that there were a number of restless spirits among the extremists of the South, that would be satisfied with nothing short of a dissolution of the Union.

Yancey's Ultimatum.

Of this class of politicians, W. L. Yancey may be fitly selected as representative man. He immediately began to agitate the question again. He went to the Democratic National Convention at Baltimore, in 1852, as a delegate from the State of Alabama, and there proposed as the *ultimatum* on which he could continue to act with the Democratic party, and upon which, in his opinion, the Slave States could consent to remain in the Union, that the doctrine of non-intervention by Congress in regard to Slavery in the Territories should be incorporated in the Democratic platform. In this he failed, and therefore did not support the nominee of the Convention, Mr. Pierce. He could not, however, at that time, succeed in creating a great schism in the Democratic party, so great had been the calm which the compromise measures of 1850 had produced. In 1856 he again went as a delegate from the State of Alabama to the Cincinnati Convention, with his old *ultimatum* in his pocket. Contrary to his wishes and expectations it was incorporated into the Cincinnati platform, and being thus left without an excuse, he supported Mr. Buchanan for the Presidency in the fall of that year.

Repeal of the Missouri Compromise.

In the mean time, however, that fatal measure, the repeal of the Missouri Compromise, had been consummated. It was brought about by the extremists of the South, aided by a few partisan Democrats at the North. The avowed object of its author was to open to Slavery the territories north of the Missouri Compromise line, notwithstanding the agreement of 1820, that said line should forever divide the territories between the Slave and Free States. It is said, however, that the compromise of 1820 was unconstitutional; but what is that to the purpose? It was a most solemn compact between the two sections of the country, made for the settlement of a most perplexing question, and, without any reference to its constitu-

tionality, should have been regarded as an organic
law, and observed as sacredly as the Constitution
itself.

The Effect of this Measure.

The effect of this measure was great and rapid, and
there can be but little doubt that it was such as a ma
jority of its authors contemplated. The result was
the formation of a great party at the North opposed
to the further extension of Slavery, and which party
very nearly succeeded in electing their candidate for
the Presidency, Mr. Fremont, in 1856. After the
election, this party seemed to be on the wane, until
the Anti-Slavery spirit of the whole North was arous
ed to madness, by an attempt on the part of Mr. Bu
chanan's Administration to *force* the Lecompton Con
stitution with Slavery upon the people of Kansas, in
opposition to the *known* and *expressed* wish of three
fourths of them. But for this most unjustifiable mea
sure, the Republican party would undoubtedly have
dwindled down to moderate proportions; and ever
after this, it is doubtful if they could have succeeded
in the Presidential election of 1860, if the Secessionists, with Yancey at their head, had not determined
that they *should* succeed. After Mr. Yancey and his
party had, against their wishes, succeeded in getting
their *ultimatum* of non-intervention incorporated into
the Cincinnati platform, they went to work to conjure
up another to present to the Charleston Convention.

Protection for Slavery demanded.

Abandoning their doctrine of non-intervention, they
went to the opposite extreme and demanded that the

:ervention of Congress for the protection of Slavery
the territories should constitute a part of the Charles-
1 platform. ' This demand they well knew would not
complied with, nor did they desire that it should be.
icir object was to procure the secession of the dele-
tes of the Cotton States from the Convention, and
1s by defeating the nomination of Mr. Douglas, and
iding asunder the Democratic party, to *insure* the elec-
n of Mr. Lincoln, and thereby *forge* for themselves
grievance which would seem to justify them in the
ecution of the long-meditated designs of destroying
: Union.　All of this they accomplished, and the
ction of Mr. Lincoln was perhaps hailed with greater
y at Charleston than at New-York.　I will do them
justice to state that they also claimed to have some
er grievances; among them, that some of the North-
States by their statutes obstructed the execution
the Fugitive Slave law, but the only States that
ild complain much on that score were willing to re-
in *in* the Union, while South-Carolina, the State
ich set the ball in motion, perhaps never lost a slave.
t it must be borne in mind that no act of the Na-
1al Government constituted any part of their griev-
es.　They did not pretend that any act of Congress
inged their rights, and the decisions of the Supreme
irt were mainly such as they would themselves
re made.　Nay, even at the very time of Mr. Lin-
a's inauguration, if the Cotton States had allowed
ir Senators and Representatives to remain, they
uld have had a decided majority in both Houses of
igress in favor of the extension of Slavery, and in
position to the policy of the party which elected
1.

The Great Cause of Complaint.

The great cause of complaint was, that a man opposed to the extension of Slavery in the Territories had been elected President of the United States, according to the forms of the Constitution, which he was sworn to defend and protect, and who disclaimed any other than constitutional means in the accomplishment of his objects. Under such circumstances it seems that if they had labored under any real grievance, their course was plain. They should have taken the course of our revolutionary fathers. When the States assembled in Convention, instead of proceeding at once to declare their independence — for the idea of secession, *peaceable of right*, seems, as Publius says, to have exploded and given up the ghost—they should clearly and concisely have stated what their grievances were, and demanded redress in respectful yet firm and decided terms. They should have exhausted *every* constitutional means of obtaining guarantees — if any were needed — by representation, by remonstrance, by petition; and failing in all these, they should have done as our revolutionary sires did, that is, fight *in the Union* for their rights until they were *driven* out of it. Such a course would have procured for us, as it did for our fathers, the respect, the sympathy, and the assistance of other nations. Instead of that, we have not a friend in Europe. But such was not the course which these — in their own estimation — wise statesmen chose to pursue. When such a course was suggested or recommended to them, they evaded it by a long list of magnificent *promises*, which looked so splendid as almost to dazzle the mind with their brilliancy.

Promises of the Secessionists.

First and foremost, they promised that secession should be *peaceable*.

Secondly. They promised that if perchance war should ensue, it would be a very *short* war; that it would not last *six* months; that the Yankees would *not* fight; that *one* Southerner could whip from *ten* to *one hundred* of them; that England and France would speedily recognize us, and render us every assistance we might desire; that whatever might be their abstract opinions of the subject of Slavery, their interests would impel them to promote its perpetuity in the Southern States; that if, after *all*, they should not be disposed to assist us, *Cotton was King*, and would soon bring *all* the crowned heads of Europe on their knees in supplication to *us ;* would compel them to raise the blockade — should one be established — in thirty days, in sixty days, in ninety days, in one hundred and twenty days, in six months, in nine months, in *one year* at furthest.

Thirdly. They *promised* us that all the Slave States except Delaware would join the Southern Confederacy; that Slavery should not only be perpetuated in the States, but that it should be extended into all the Territories in which the negro could live ; that all the grievances occasioned by the non-execution of the Fugitive Slave Law should be speedily redressed ; that slave property should be established upon a basis as safe as that of landed property.

Fourthly. They *promised* us that the new government should be a mere Confederacy of States, of absolute sovereignty and equal rights; that the States should be tyrannized over by *no* such *"central despotism"* as the old Government at Washington; that the glorious doctrine of State rights and nullification, as taught by Mr. Jefferson and Mr. Calhoun, should prevail in the new Confederacy; that the *sovereignty* of the States and their judicial decisions should be sacredly respected.

Fifthly. They *promised* us the early and permanent establishment of the wealthiest and best government on the earth, whose *credit* should be better than that of any other nation; whose prosperity and happiness should be the envy of the civilized world.

And lastly, they *promised* us that if war *should* ensue, *they* would go to the battle-field, and spill, if necessary, the *last* drop of their blood in the cause of their beloved South.

Performances of the Secessionists.

While such have been their *promises*, what have been their *performances?* Instead of secession being peaceable, as they promised that it would, it has given rise to such a war as has never before desolated any country, since the barbarians of the North overran the Roman Empire.

So far from the war's ending in six months, as they said it would, should it ensue, it has already lasted more than two years; and if their policy is to be pursued, it will last more than two years longer; and, notwithstanding their predictions, the Yankees have fought on many occasions with a spirit and determination worthy of their ancestors of the Revolution — worthy of the descendants of those austere old Puritans whose heroic spirit and religious zeal made Oliver Cromwell's army the terror of the civilized world — or of those French Huguenots, "who, thrice in the sixteenth century, contended with heroic spirit and various fortunes against all the genius of the house of Lorraine, and all the power of the house of Valois." England and France have not recognized us — have not raised the blockade — have not shown us any sympathy, nor is there any probability that they ever will; and that Cotton is *not* King, is now universally acknowledged. And Maryland has *not* joined the Confederacy, nor has Kentucky nor Missouri ever really been with us. Slavery has not only not been perpetuated in the States, nor extended into the Territories, but Missouri has passed an act of *emancipation*, and Maryland is ready to do so rather than give up her place in the Union, and the *last* hope of obtaining one foot of the Territories for the purpose of extending Slavery has departed from the Confederacy *forever*. The grievances caused by the failure of some of the Northern States to execute the Fugitive Slave Law, have not only not been remedied, but more slaves have been lost to the South forever since secession was inaugurated, than would have escaped from their masters *in* the Union in five centuries. And how have they kept their promise that they would respect the sovereignty and rights of the States? Whatever the Government may be in *theory*, in *fact* we have a grand military *consolidation*, which almost entirely ignores the existence of the States, and disregards the decisions of their highest judicial tribunals. The great central despotism at Washington, as they were pleased to call it, was at any time previous to the commencement of the secession movement, and even for some time after it had commenced, a most mild and beneficent Government compared with the *central despotism* at Richmond, under which we are now living.

What have we got?

Instead of an early and permanent establishment of the "wealthiest and best government in the world, with unbounded credit," what have we got? In spite of all the victories which they profess to have obtained over the Yankees, they have lost the States of Missouri, Kentucky, Arkansas, Texas, Louisiana, Mississippi, and Tennessee, and in my humble opinion have lost them forever; and, in all probability, Alabama will soon be added to the number. This will leave to the Confederacy but *five* States out of the original thirteen, and of these five the Yankees have possession of many of the most important points, and one third of their territory. So far, the Yankees have never failed to hold every place of importance which they have taken, and present indications are, that Charleston will soon be added to the number. The campaign of General Lee into Pennsylvania has undoubtedly proved a failure, and with it the last hope of conquering a peace by a successful invasion of the enemy's country. Our army has certainly been very much weakened and dispirited by this failure and the fall of Vicksburgh, and how long even Richmond will be safe no one can tell. As the Richmond *Enquirer* said some time ago, "They are slowly but *surely* gaining upon us acre by acre, mile by mile," and, unless Providence interposes in our behalf — of which I see no indications — we will, at no great distance of time, be a subjugated people.

As to our unbounded credit based upon the security of King Cotton, it is unnecessary to speak. When we see one of the most influential States in the Confederacy discrediting a very large part of the confederate currency, and the confederate government itself repudiating, to some extent, its most solemn obligations, we can not but suppose that the confidence of other nations in the good faith and credit of this government is small indeed. As regards their promise " to go to the war and spill the last drop of their blood in the cause of their beloved South," I will say nothing. Every body knows how the Secessionists of North-Carolina have kept that promise. Every body knows that the leaders, with a few honorable exceptions, will neither fight nor negotiate.

No Guarantees demanded by the South.

What a deplorable spectacle does the foregoing history present to our view! To what a desperate pass have they brought us, and for what? They say that they did it because the North would give us no guarantee in the Slavery question. I have before stated that not one of the Conventions of the seven Cotton States ever demanded any guarantee whatever. Nay, they even refused to accept of any if their friends of the Border States would procure it for them.

The Legislature of North-Carolina, at its regular session in January, 1861, adopted resolutions appointing Commissioners to the Peace Congress at Washington City, and also to the Convention which assembled at Montgomery, Alabama, in February, 1861, for the purpose of adopting a Constitution, and establishing a provisional government for the confederate States of America. On the motion of the writer of this, the resolution appointing Commissioners to Montgomery was amended so as to instruct them " to act only as *mediators*, and use every effort possible to restore the Union upon the basis of the *Crittenden propositions as modified by the Legislature of Virginia.*" The Commissioners under these instructions were the Hon. D. L. Swan, General M. W. Ransom, and John L. Bridgers, Esq., who, upon their return, submitted a report to his Excellency, Gov. Ellis, which was by him laid before the Legislature, and was printed among the legislative documents of that year, where it may be consulted. In this report they say that they had the most ample opportunities of ascertaining public opinion in the Cotton States, and then add: " We regret to be constrained to state, as the result of our inquiries, made under such circumstances, that only a very *decided minority* of the community in these States are disposed at present, to entertain favorably, *any* proposition of adjustment which looks toward a reconstruction of our National Union. In this state of things we have not deemed it our duty to attend any of the secret sessions of the Congress. The resolutions of the General Assembly are upon the table of the Congress, and having submitted them as a peace-offering, we would poorly perform the duties assigned to us by entering into discussions which would serve only to enkindle strife."

But it will be said that these guarantees could not

have been obtained from the North.   This I admit to
be true, and only produce this piece of history to
prove that whatever might have been obtained, nothing would have been accepted.   But the Congress of
the United States did pass, by the constitutional majority of two thirds, the proposition reported by Mr.
Corwin, from the Committee of twenty-six, to so amend
the Constitution as to *perpetuate* slavery in the States.
What stronger guarantees could be given so far as the
States were concerned it would be difficult to conceive.
What then would have been left to quarrel about?
The Territories.   During the session of Congress which
closed on the fourth of March, 1861, acts were passed
to provide temporary governments for the three re-
maining new Territories, to wit, Colorado, Nevada,
and Dacotah.   These acts contain no trace or indica-
tion of the Wilmot Proviso, nor any other prohibition
against the introduction of Slavery, but on the other
hand, expressly declare among other things, that " no
law shall be passed impairing the rights of private property : nor shall any discrimination be made in taxing
different kinds of property, but all property subject to
taxation shall be in proportion to the value of the property taxed."

Nothing to Quarrel About.

Now, when it is considered that all three of these
Territories are *north* of 36° 30', and that in the new
Territory now owned by the United States *south* of that
line *Slavery actually exists and is recognized by the ter-
ritorial law,* the question may well be asked : " What
was there worth quarrelling, much less fighting about?"
Here was a settlement of the question in the Territo-

ries made by a Republican Congress, which gave the South all that up to the time of the Charleston Convention she had ever asked, and far more than she could hope to gain, in any event, by secession — indeed, I think it must now be apparent that secession, even if it could have been effected peaceably, would have been *no* remedy for the grievances of which they complained. Nay, so far as any grievances arising from a failure to obtain a return of our fugitive slaves was concerned, I think it must now be apparent that it would have been an aggravation instead of a remedy for the evil. I think all calm and dispassionate men everywhere are now ready to admit that it would have been far better for us to have accepted the terms offered to us and preserved *peace* and the Union, than to have plunged this once happy country into the horrors of this desolating war, which has spread a pall over the whole land — has brought mourning into every family—has rendered hundreds of thousands of hearth-stones desolate—has filled the land with maimed and disabled, with widows and orphans, and squalid poverty—has crowded our poorhouses and almshouses — has sported away many hundreds of thousands of lives and many hundreds of millions of treasure, only to find the institution for which they profess to have gone to war in a thousand times greater jeopardy than ever before.

Is there any Remedy?

Such being the condition into which they have brought the country, the question presents itself, " Is there any remedy?" A full, complete, and adequate remedy there is not; for what can restore the loved ones lost—repair at once the desolation, or remove immediately the mourning from our land? Yet there is a remedy, which, with the helping hand of time, will accomplish much, very much indeed, and which, with the energy that usually follows desolating wars, will, perhaps, remove most of its traces in a half-century. This remedy is *peace*, SPEEDY PEACE! But they say that we are so situated that *no* proposition for peace can be made by us; that having proclaimed our independence we *must* fight until it is voluntarily acknowledged by the United States, or until we are *completely subjugated*. On the meeting of the British Parliament, which took place on the thirteenth of December, 1792, the King in his speech to the two Houses, intimated his intention of going to war with the French Republic. On moving the address in answer to the speech, a memorable debate arose. On this occasion Charles James Fox delivered one of those powerful speeches which have made his name immortal—which have forever stamped him as the ablest of British debaters and the first of British statesmen. In the course of that speech he said: "But we now disdain to negotiate. Why? Because we have no Minister at Paris. Why have we no Minister there? Because France is a Republic! And so we are to pay in blood and treasure of the people for a *punctilio!* . . . The road of common-sense is simple, plain, and direct. That of *pride* and *punctilio* is as tangled as it is serpentine." In the impassioned language of Mr. Fox, I would ask, are we to pay in blood and treasure of the people for a *punctilio?* Shall we pursue the path of pride and punctilio, which is as tangled as it is serpentine, or shall we take the simple, plain, and direct road of com-

mon-sense, which may lead to the happiest results?
Four fifths of the people of that portion of North-Carolina bordering for many miles on the Yadkin River,
and I believe of the whole State, are in favor of the
latter' course.

Demand for Peace.

The one great demand of the *people* of this part of
the State is *peace ; peace* upon any terms that will not
enslave and degrade us. They may, perhaps, prefer
that the independence of the South should be acknowledged, but this they believe can not now be obtained,
nor in viewing the situation of affairs, do they see much
to hope of it in the future. They naturally ask, if
with no means of recruiting to any extent, we can not
hold our own against the armies which the Yankees
have now in the field, how can we meet them with
their three hundred thousand new levies which will
soon be in readiness, while they can keep their army
recruited to a great extent, if not up to its *maximum*
number, from adventurers which are constantly arriv-
ing in their ports from every country in Europe? But
if independence can not be obtained, then they are for
any terms that are honorable — any terms that do not
degrade us. They would be willing to compromise
upon the amendment proposed by Mr. Corwin from
the Committee of Twenty-six, perpetuating Slavery in
the States to which I have before alluded. But in
what precise way overtures shall be made, or the movement inaugurated, I leave to wiser men and abler
statesmen than myself to propose. I would, however,
suggest to the people to elect members to the next
Congress, who are in favor of an armistice of six
months, and in the mean time, of submitting all mat-

ters in dispute to a Convention of delegates from all the States North and South, *the delegates to be elected by the people themselves*, in such manner as may be agreed upon by the two parties. Others there are, who desire that the people of North-Carolina should be consulted in their sovereign capacity through a convention—that the Legislature should submit the question of " Convention or no Convention " to the people, as was done in February, 1861. Such a convention would undoubtedly speak the sentiments of the people of the State, citizens as well as soldiers, as all would be consulted. But I propose nothing definite, and only make these suggestions to bring the matter before the public. I would, however, most earnestly appeal to the friends of humanity throughout the State to use their utmost efforts to procure as speedily as possible an *honorable peace*. In the name of reason, of suffering humanity, and of the religion which we profess would I appeal to the public men and statesmen of North-Carolina, and especially to that eminent statesman who possesses in a greater degree than all others the confidence of the people of the State, and who has recently been elevated to a high place in the confederate government, to lend a helping hand and use their influence to bring about an *honorable peace*. And lastly, I would appeal to the ministers and professors of our holy religion to pray constantly — without dictation of terms — to Almighty God for an *honorable peace*.

Having but recently occupied a large space in your columns, I feel that I am intruding, and will therefore, after expressing my obligations to you, close for the present. DAVIDSON.

CLEMONSVILLE, N. C., July 16, 1863.

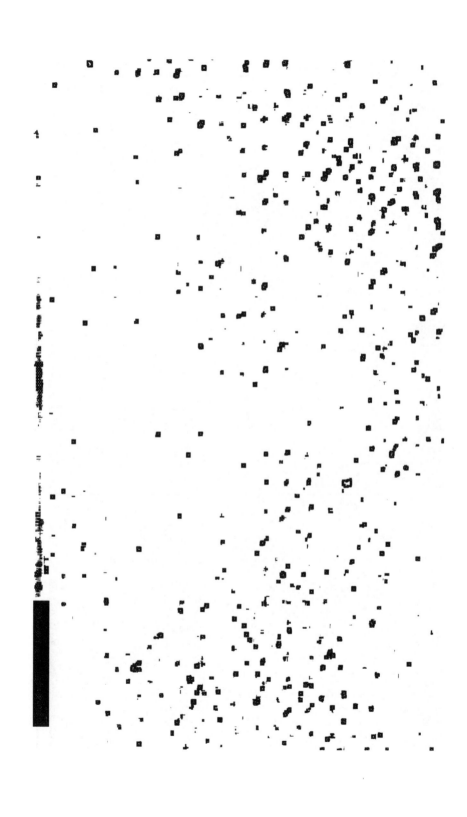

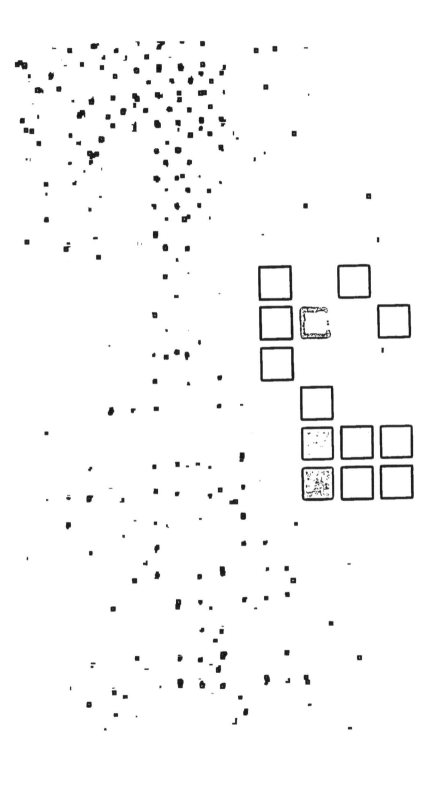

Lightning Source UK Ltd.
Milton Keynes UK
UKHW022100250822
407860UK00003BA/122

9 781363 920846